REVOLUTIONS

BELIEFS AND IDEAS
that changed the world

CLARE HIBBERT

BRITISH LIBRARY

First published 2017 by
The British Library
96 Euston Road
London NW1 2DB

Text © Clare Hibbert 2017
Illustrations © The British Library Board
and other named copyright-holders 2017

ISBN 978 0 7123 5680 0

British Library Cataloguing in Publication Data
A catalogue record for this publication is available
from the British Library

Designed by Amy McSimpson @ Hollow Pond
Picture research by Sally Nicholls

Printed in Malta by Gutenberg Press Ltd.

BELIEFS AND IDEAS
that changed the world

REVOLUTIONS

INTRODUCTION

It is 65,000 years since our species, *Homo sapiens*, spread out from Africa. Even then, we already had some simple spiritual beliefs. We know this from very early burials. Over our long history, we humans have come up with complex religions, epic stories and awesome scientific explanations. This book looks at a few of the most interesting ones along our journey.

The story of the Greeks sneaking into Troy in a wooden horse is made up, but the war itself almost certainly happened.

EXPLAINING LIFE

Beliefs and ideas often set out to explain mysteries, such as what makes an animal behave the way it does, why the landscape is shaped how it is, or where we go when we die. Some stories present a mix of truth and fiction. Others are pure fact or pure fiction.

Many cultures tell of a great flood. There is some evidence there really was one, too.

Darwin's theory of evolution turned the world upside-down. People were horrified at the idea of humans and other apes being related.

IMPROVING LIFE

Throughout history, new beliefs and ideas have created new ways to run our societies. They have brought in improvements ... and they have also sometimes ended in disaster. In the same way, religious beliefs have changed people's behaviour both for good and bad.

Religious differences between Christians and Muslims caused wars called Crusades in the Middle Ages.

Islamic scholars have increased our understanding in many fields, including astronomy and maths.

Campaigners for women's rights made education available to girls in most places.

The thinker Ka
Marx develop
Communism
way of sha
ownershi
life faire

VIP These boxes introduce
very important peopl
history of religion a

NEED TO KNOW

Find out key facts and dates in these box

MARVELLOUS MYTHS

Myths and legends are the oldest stories there are. Since earliest times, people have told them to explain big ideas - and also because they're fun to listen to. Myths are passed on to the next generations by being spoken aloud or written down. Sometimes they are expressed in other ways - through songs, dances or art.

MYSTERIOUS POWERS

Myths often feature superhuman beings that possess greater powers than ordinary mortals. They might be gods or spirits. Some stories that we now think of as myths were part of ancient religions. In civilisations ancient Egypt and Greece, tales monsters and heroes formed the everyday behaviour, worship.

you to from the and ideas.

many

for all.

This page shows the Aztec creator g
Tezcatlipoca (left) and Quetzalcoatl (
Most cultures around the world have
to explain how everything was

IN THE BEGINNING ...

How did we get here? That was one of the first questions that early people wondered about ... once they had time to think about more than the next meal! Just about every culture and religion on Earth has a story to explain the creation.

This is the Egyptian sun god, Re, crossing the sky on the first day.

The Egyptians thought the earth god held up the newly made world and the sky goddess arched over it.

Nut, goddess of the sky

Scarab beetle, the symbol of creation

Geb, god of the earth

Nun, the god of watery chaos

...ods ...ght). ...tories ...s made.

Quetzalcoatl, the feathered serpent, was one of the Aztec creator gods.

...ve birth ...gods, who ...everything. They ...ented north, south, ...and west. Quetzalcoatl ...was the god of the east.

Some of the creator gods became sun gods. They ruled over the Earth during different ages. Quetzalcoatl was the second sun god.

OUTSIDE TIME

The Aboriginal people of Australia believe that past, present and future all exist at the same time. The great spirits created everything during a time in the past called the Dreaming.

WOW!

In some myths, the world hatches out of a magical egg, called the cosmic egg.

Aboriginal people believe that the great spirits created Uluru, also known as Ayers Rock, at the beginning of time.

BIRD OF THE BEGINNING

The Haida people of America's Pacific Northwest say that Raven found the first people in a clam shell. They also say that he brought light and water into the world. As well as being a creator, Raven is a trickster in the myths of many Native American tribes.

A Haida print of Raven, the creator

REVOLUTIONS

In most stories, only chaos exists in the time before the creation, and the world itself is made long before the people. These simple ideas helped people to understand their beginnings, and we now know they also contained some truth.

DASHING HEROES

Many myths tell of strong, brave heroes. Sometimes, like the Greek hero Perseus, they are demigods (Perseus's father was the god Zeus). They often go on a dangerous journey to defeat a monster or find something precious. By their actions, they change things for ordinary people.

Perseus chopped off the head of a monster called Medusa. On his way home, he rescued a princess.

A sea serpent was holding Princess Andromeda prisoner.

Dead dragon

Medusa had snakes for hair and her gaze could kill.

PERSEVS RESCVES ANDROMEDA

WOW!

The Romans adapted their favourite Greek stories to star their own heroes. Hercules was based on the Greek demigod, Heracles.

The Greek hero Jason went on a quest to find the Golden Fleece.

 **VIP** The Roman hero Hercules had to carry out 12 brave deeds so he could become immortal like his father, the god Jupiter.

NEED TO KNOW

Roman demigod Hercules killed a lion, slayed a many-headed monster called the Hydra, caught a golden deer and trapped a fearsome boar.

Next, Hercules cleaned out some mucky stables, shot down man-eating birds, tamed a bull and stole some flesh-eating horses.

Hercules' last four tasks were stealing a queen's belt, taking a giant's cattle, pinching some magic apples and kidnapping a three-headed dog!

NEW BEGINNINGS

When heroes return from their adventures, they may start new cities or civilisations. In Greek myths, Perseus founded the kingdom of Mycenae, while Jason became king of Iolcos. The Mesopotamian hero-god Marduk was said to have built Eridu, the world's oldest city.

Marduk

Marduk destroyed a goddess called Tiamat.

Tiamat, the goddess of chaos

King Arthur

The Green Knight, an immortal

Gawain has chopped off the Green Knight's head – and agreed to have the same done to himself the following year.

TALES OF COURAGE

In Britain, people told legends about a courageous king called Arthur who protected them from invaders. His loyal Knights of the Round Table were very brave, too.

Sir Gawain, one of Arthur's knights, accepted a terrifying challenge from the Green Knight.

REVOLUTIONS

In early societies, leaders had to be successful warriors. They were treated almost like gods. The amazing feats of mythical heroes helped people to understand this through stories.

TRICKSTERS

Not all myths are about brave heroes. Tricksters are sneaky, clever characters that appear in stories from around the world. They have to rely on their wits because they are not strong or courageous. Tricksters are only out for themselves, and definitely not to be trusted!

In Norse mythology, the god Loki was always switching sides and playing tricks.

Loki teased his brother Thor, the Norse god of thunder. But sometimes the two teamed up against the giants.

NEED TO KNOW

VIP The Ashanti people of Ghana say that Anansi is a protector of stories and wisdom.

Anansi is a trickster from West African stories. African slaves took their stories with them when they were transported overseas, so Anansi also appears in Caribbean folklore.

Anansi is part-human and part-spider. In some illustrations, he looks just like a spider. In others, he might be a spider with human features or a human with spider features.

The most famous Anansi tale is about him bringing stories to Earth. The sky god asked a high price for them but Anansi paid it — thanks to clever trickery, of course!

WILY COYOTE

In Native American myths Coyote, like Raven, is sometimes a creator and sometimes a trickster. He is always stealing and lying. Like the Norse god Loki, Coyote is said to have stolen fire from the gods for humankind.

Many different Native American tribes have stories about Coyote.

WOW!

In Aztec mythology, coyotes were brave, not cowardly.

SNEAKY FOXES

Like real coyotes and ravens, foxes are scavengers. Perhaps that is why they also appear as untrustworthy tricksters in some cultures. Reynard the Fox stars in stories from northern Europe. He dresses like a person and uses sneaky tricks to raid farmers' poultry.

Reynard has disguised himself as a vicar to get close to the geese.

In Japan, *kitsune* are magical, shape-shifting foxes.

REVOLUTIONS

Trickster tales helped people to understand how cleverness could be just as useful as strength. Some stories explain the origins of much-loved comforts, such as fire or stories.

✗✗✗✗✗✗✗✗✗✗✗✗✗✗✗✗✗✗

SCARY MONSTERS

Lots of stories have monsters. Being wild and savage, they show us what we would be like if we did not behave like human beings. They can even take the blame for disasters. People like the excitement of being scared when, deep down, they know that it is only a story.

Long ago, when lives were lost at sea, people sometimes said it was the fault of supernatural sea monsters.

The ferocious Minotaur of Greek myth is half-bull. Because it is not properly human, it does terrible things, such as eat young people.

NEED TO KNOW

VIP

In Greek myth, a harpy had a bird's body and a woman's head.

Many monsters are hybrids (mixes) of different animals. In Indian stories, the makara is a monster that usually has a fishy tail but its front half is a land animal, such as a stag, elephant or crocodile.

Like the Minotaur, many hybrids are part-human. Werewolves can change from a person into wolf form and back again.

The Chinese qilin had a dragon's head, deer's antlers, fishy scales, ox's hooves and a lion's tail!

GIANT BEASTS

Dragons appear in many cultures. Perhaps people told tales about them after finding dinosaur fossils, and not knowing what they were. Sightings of sea serpents might have really been glimpses of creatures such as giant squid.

This water dragon appears on a 17th-century Japanese scroll.

Dragons are usually winged and scaly. They can sometimes breathe fire.

WOW!

In Chinese culture, dragons are lucky.

Beowulf killing Grendel's mother

MAKING THINGS BETTER

When heroes defeat monsters, they bring back order. The Old English hero Beowulf killed a beast called Grendel – and then went and killed its mother, too, in her underwater lair.

REVOLUTIONS

Monsters in stories give listeners a thrill. They can represent scary ideas such as chaos or violence. When a monster is defeated, listeners feel satisfied and safe again.

DISASTROUS DESTRUCTION

Natural disasters such as floods, earthquakes and volcanoes claim lives and cause terrible damage. Today, we understand how and why they happen. Long ago, people made up stories to explain them. They often thought these terrible events were some sort of punishment.

One Japanese myth tells how earthquakes happen because of a huge, mischievous catfish called Namazu.

LA MER

Namazu was said to cause tsunamis (tidal waves), too.

Poseidon triggered earthquakes by banging his trident.

NEED TO KNOW

VIP

In the stories of the Maori people of New Zealand, earthquakes and volcanoes happen because of the earth goddess's baby son, Ruaumoko.

In Chinese mythology, the world rests on the back of a giant frog. When the frog twitches, Earth shakes and there are earthquakes and tremors.

The ancient Greeks said their god of the sea, Poseidon, caused earthquakes. He did it to punish people or simply because he was angry.

DESTRUCTIVE ERUPTIONS

The Romans thought volcanoes happened because of the god Vulcan working metal in his forge. The Hawaiians blamed their fire goddess Pele for them. In Indonesia, people still throw gifts of money or even live animals into volcanoes to try to calm them.

Mount Merapi is one of Indonesia's most active volcanoes. Its name means 'fire mountain'.

FEARFUL FLOODS

Floods bring destruction. There is a flood in the earliest surviving written tale, the *Epic of Gilgamesh*. Flood stories were also told in India, China, Mexico and Australia. Sometimes there is a survivor, who has been chosen by the gods.

WOW!

The *Epic of Gilgamesh* was inscribed into clay tablets in Mesopotamia (ancient Iraq) more than 4,000 years ago.

In stories, floods are usually sent to punish people.

In the Old Testament story of the Flood, Noah builds a boat. He saves himself and all the animals.

REVOLUTIONS

Once people believed their actions caused disasters, the next step was obvious. They had to be good, perform special rituals or give gifts to the gods.

△△△△△△△△△△△△

LIFE AFTER DEATH

Many myths explain what happens to us after death. The ancient Egyptians believed that the dead travelled to another world, where they would need their bodies and even their belongings. It was called the Field of Reeds, and there was plenty to eat and drink there.

Osiris's sister, the goddess Nephthys

Osiris's wife, the goddess Isis

Osiris, god of the dead and the underworld, being embalmed

Jackal-headed Anubis, Egyptian god of mummy-making

Egyptian mummies were buried in decorative cases, along with lucky charms called amulets.

NEED TO KNOW

VIP

Green-skinned Osiris was the Egyptian god of the dead.

Some rich Egyptians were buried with instruction manuals for their journey to the afterlife. These are called Books of the Dead.

The important part of the journey was when Anubis weighed the dead person's heart. If it balanced the feather of truth, the person could go to the Field of Reeds.

If the heart outweighed the feather, it was proof of a wicked life. The dead person would be devoured by a monster. This time, they died forever.

VIKING VISION

In Norse mythology, dead heroes went to a great hall called Valhalla. For them, it was paradise. They drank and feasted there with Odin, god of death and war.

Vikings believed in nine different worlds. Valhalla was in Asgard, a world of the gods.

Einherjar (warriors who died in battle)

Odin with one of his wolves

GREEN GARDEN

The Aztecs believed in a garden paradise where people went after death. Their idea of it might seem strange to us because there are human sacrifices. The Aztec storm god, Tlaloc, looked after the garden. Earlier Central American peoples had worshipped Tlaloc, too.

The different worlds in Norse myth were connected by a magical ash tree, Yggdrasil.

This mural of Tlaloc's garden is from the city of Teotihuacán. It shows people working and playing.

WOW!

Dead warriors were carried to Valhalla by winged goddesses called valkyries.

Humans are being sacrificed to the mountain. In return, the mountain provides streams to water the crops.

REVOLUTIONS

Myths about the afterlife gave people clues about how to behave while they were alive. They could help to ensure a good afterlife by being brave or making sacrifices.

MANY GODS

The oldest religions involve the worship of many gods. Each god looks after one aspect of existence, such as an emotion, action or place. People pray or make offerings to different gods according to their needs. They may ask for a good harvest, a healthy baby or protection from disaster.

BORROWED REALITY

Believing in many gods is called polytheism. Some polytheistic religions, such as those of ancient Greece and Rome, have died out. Others, such as Hinduism, are still going strong today. These gods are not afraid of action. They take part in huge battles that mimic real-life perils and difficulties. Their stories teach people how to overcome dangers, and who or what to trust.

The homes of the gods can be real places. The Greek gods were said to live on Mount Olympus. This Buddhist illustration shows the paradise-like realm of Himavant. Loosely based on the Himalayas, it is home to gods, demons and wild animals.

There are many epic struggles in the stories of Hindu gods. Here, the ogre Sukesha's sons set off to fight Vishnu and his army.

FOLK RELIGIONS

Folk religions have stories that explain creation and many gods or spirits that can bring help or trouble. Many of them have died out in modern times. We know about them from artefacts such as statues and masks, or from paintings or photographs.

This painting shows Lakota warriors dancing before a bear hunt to please the Bear Spirit. It is by the 19th-century American artist George Catlin.

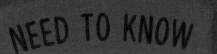

This photo of 1912 shows a ritual dance by the Nupe people of Nigeria. The two tall figures represent the male and female aspects of one of their great spirits, the Dako-Boea.

NEED TO KNOW

 VIP

The 19th-century anthropologist Edward Tylor coined the term animism to describe the belief in spirits being everywhere.

Prehistoric burials suggest that early humans had spiritual beliefs and rituals as long as **300,000** years ago.

The spread of major religions such as Christianity and Islam stamped out traditional folk beliefs in many parts of the world.

Folk religions live on in remote parts of the world. In these places, a medicine man or shaman is the link between the tribe and the spirits.

AMAZING ARTEFACTS

Traditional societies often have no written language. They pass on stories through word of mouth. They also express spiritual ideas through their art. Objects have a religious meaning.

The Yoruba people of Nigeria wear carved 'spirit masks' for some rituals. The wearer takes on the powers of the spirit.

Native Americans of the Pacific Northwest carved spirit world stories onto colourful totem poles.

MODERN MYSTICS

Some peoples hold on to their traditional beliefs because they have little contact with the outside world. In other places, people keep traditions and rituals alive in order to appeal to tourists.

WOW!

The Yanomami people live in the Amazon rainforest. In 2016 aerial photos were released of a Yanomami village that had never had contact with the outside world.

A Siberian shaman beats his drum to contact the spirit world.

REVOLUTIONS

Folk religions usually involve powerful rituals. These help people to get in touch with their spiritual side. Many of the tricks practised by ancient shamans, such as using rhythmic, repetitive music, still work on us today.

SACRED INDIAN TEXTS

Together, holy Hindu writings are known as the *Shruti* ('that which is heard'). They include the hymns, prayers and chants in the four *Vedas*, written between 1200 and 900 BCE, as well as philosophical teachings, myths (the *Puranas*) and epic poems. They are written in Sanskrit, the ancient language of India.

This 18th-century watercolour shows the god Rama with the goddess Radha.

The many-armed goddess Durga, wife of the god Shiva

VIP

The three great gods are Brahma, Vishnu and Shiva. Vishnu has ten different forms, or avatars, including Krishna (right).

NEED TO KNOW

Hinduism dates back to India's first civilisation — the people who built the cities of Mohenjo-Daro and Harappa in the Indus Valley around **2500** BCE.

In Hinduism, there is one supreme being, Brahman, a holy trio of three great gods and countless minor gods.

By **1500** BCE, Hindu beliefs had spread throughout northern India.

HEART OF HINDUISM

Vishnu is the Hindu god who preserves human life. He has ten avatars. As Krishna, his words make up the *Bhagavad Gita*, a song at the heart of the *Mahabharata*, which was written around 500 BCE. The song is a conversation between Krishna and his chariot driver, Arjuna. Most of the *Mahabharata* is about a feud between two families.

Krishna is often shown with blue skin

WOW!

The Mahabharata is the longest poem in the world, consisting of more than 220,000 verses, or 1.8 million words.

THE RAMAYANA

Written around 300 BCE, the *Ramayana* tells the story of Vishnu's seventh avatar, Rama. He must rescue his wife Sita, who has been kidnapped by Ravana, demon king of Lanka. The monkey god Hanuman helps Rama to defeat Ravana.

Rama's brother, Lakshmana

Rama riding Hanuman

Monkey army

Hanuman about to throw a rock

Ravana's son, Indrajit

These two illustrations are from a 17th-century *Ramayana*.

REVOLUTIONS

Some Hindu writings, including the Vedas, are divine, so not a word can be changed. Their message is the same to all 1.1 million Hindus around the world.

HINDU TEMPLES AND WORSHIP

Most Hindu homes have their own shrine, where the family worships its favourite gods each day. Hindus also visit temples to take part in services led by priests called Brahmin. There are special Hindu festivals, including Holi in spring and Diwali, the October festival of lights.

An 18th-century painting of a Hindu temple in Thanjavur, southern India, that was built more than 1,000 years ago.

Many Hindus practise yoga, because it exercises the body, mind and spirit.

One of the three great gods, Shiva is also known as the destroyer.

NEED TO KNOW

Hindus pray by repeating sacred poems or mantras. They also chant the word OM, meaning 'god'. The humming sound helps them to feel closer to the gods.

Shivaratri is a popular Hindu festival that honours the god Shiva. It takes place in February or March.

Shiva is believed to live in Varanasi in northern India. Many Hindus go on pilgrimages to the city.

FABULOUS FESTIVALS

There are Hindu celebrations throughout the year. Thousands visit Puri in eastern India each year to see Ratha-Yatra, the Chariot Festival. Chariots transport icons of the god Jagannath and his brother and sister from one temple to another. Nine days later, they make the journey back again.

Ratha-Yatra being celebrated in Puri

WOW!

Our English word 'juggernaut' comes from the huge, unstoppable chariot that carries the god Jagannath.

Each of the three chariots is decorated to look like a temple.

PILGRIMAGES

The holy city of Varanasi sits on the banks of the Ganges river. Pilgrims bathe in the river to purify themselves. They also go there to cremate loved ones or scatter their ashes.

This is how Varanasi looked in 1901.

Pilgrims stand on stone jetties called *ghats*.

According to stories, the Ganges spouted from Shiva's head.

REVOLUTIONS

Every Hindu belongs to one of four varnas (classes): priests/ teachers, rulers/ warriors, farmers/ merchants or servants/ labourers. India's caste system is based on these.

THE BUDDHA'S TEACHINGS

Buddhism began around 450 BCE. It is based on the teachings of Siddhartha Gautama, a prince who lived in northeast India. He gave up his rich life and went on a quest to find contentment. He became known as the Buddha, or 'Enlightened One'.

The Buddha reached a state of peace and knowledge called enlightenment. He was meditating under a tree.

This 18th-century image of the Buddha comes from Thailand.

 Siddhartha Gautama lived from around 485 BCE to 405 BCE.

NEED TO KNOW

At the heart of the Buddha's teachings were Four Noble Truths. The first was that people cannot be satisfied with life.

The second truth explained that people are discontented because they want things to stay the same, but that is not possible.

The third truth was that people could be content by reaching nirvana. The fourth explained how to reach it by following eight simple steps.

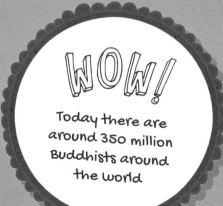

THE SPREAD OF BUDDHISM

After his enlightenment, the Buddha travelled around with a small group of disciples. Buddhism spread across India and into nearby countries. It probably reached China in the 200s BCE and Japan in the 500s CE.

This bronze statue of the Buddha dates to around 1252. It stands beside a Buddhist temple in the coastal city of Kamakura, Japan.

WOW!

Today there are around 350 million Buddhists around the world

SACRED PLACES

There are different styles of Buddhist temple in different places. Stupas are ancient burial mounds that contain relics of early Buddhists or even the Buddha himself. Buddhists visit them to meditate. Pagodas are temples with many tiers.

This 19th-century watercolour shows a Buddhist pagoda in Nepal.

Burma's most sacred Buddhist temple is the stupa at Yangon, shown here in an engraving from 1825.

Temple is festooned with mementoes of the dead.

The stupa is gilded (coated in gold).

REVOLUTIONS

Buddhism has been a strong influence in the East. In many countries, boys still spend some of their youth living as monks in a Buddhist monastery. The religion values kindness and calm.

TRADITIONAL BELIEFS IN CHINA

Different belief systems live side by side in China, and people take elements from them all. In addition to Buddhism, many Chinese people follow Confucianism, Taoism and folk religion. Some ideas, such as finding balance between opposing forces, appear in all three.

Taoism was founded by the scholar Lao-Tzu in the 6th century BCE.

Oracle bone (16th to 10th century BCE)

Since ancient times, the Chinese had used oracle bones to try to divine (work out) the future.

There are many gods in Taoism, but three supreme ones.

NEED TO KNOW

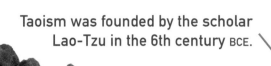

VIP

Confucius lived from 551 BCE to 479 BCE.

Confucius was a teacher and philosopher. He drew on ancient books, such as the I Ching (c. 3000 BCE), to come up with a code for living.

Confucius encouraged people to carry on with traditional practices, such as worshipping their ancestors and reading oracle bones.

Followers of Confucius can believe in any god or no god at all. The important thing is to do their duty and be part of a stable, respectful society.

TAOIST IMMORTALS

Lao-Tzu believed that it was possible to achieve immortality (eternal life). People needed to follow the Tao (the Way) by meditating, chanting and doing physical exercise, such as tai chi.

The immortal Wise Mother of Dongling rises on a cloud.

The immortal Huang Renlan rides a dragon to heaven.

WOW!

Confucius, Lao-Tzu and the Buddha were all alive at the same time.

These 18th-century paintings show followers of the Tao who achieved immortality, or tried to.

The Eight Immortals were characters from Chinese mythology who had found a way to live forever.

YIN AND YANG

For the Chinese, yin represents all that is female, cold, dark, below and soft. Yang is everything male, hot, light, above and hard. Together, these opposites make a powerful whole – but if they are not in balance, they can cause sickness.

This door sign kept out evil spirits.

Yin and yang symbol

REVOLUTIONS

Confucianism helped to create an ordered society, with loyalty to the emperor. Even after the Communists took over China in the 20th century, Confucian values of working and studying hard remained strong.

✕✕✕✕✕✕✕✕✕✕✕✕✕✕✕✕

THE WAY OF THE GODS

Japan's traditional religion is Shinto, whose name means the 'way of the gods'. Followers believe that there are thousands of *kami* (gods and spirits) that watch over people and things. They live in the landscape, inside mountains, trees, rocks and rivers.

Temples were built in natural settings, close to the gods. Here, a monk meditates in a temple next to a waterfall.

The entrance to Shinto shrines and some Buddhist temples in Japan is a special gate, called a torii. It can be red and black or unpainted.

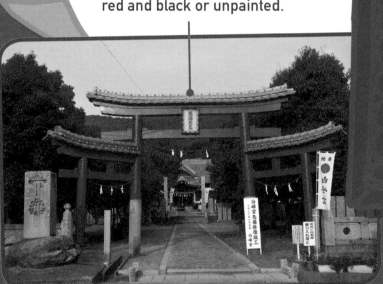

In Shinto mythology, Amaterasu is the supreme deity.

NEED TO KNOW

VIP

Most of the gods and spirits honoured in Shinto appear in two books, the Kojiki and the Nihonshoki. Both were written in the 700s CE.

In Shinto, the gods Izanagi and Izanami created the islands of Japan. They dipped a spear into the sea and let the drops of salt water form land.

Izanagi and Izanami had a daughter, the sun goddess Amaterasu. She brought light and order into the world.

SHINTO SHRINES

Shrines are sacred spaces. Worshippers enter through the torii gate. They wash their hands and mouth before they go into the prayer hall. Beyond the prayer hall is a hall where the *kami* lives. Only priests can go into this area.

This 17th-century scroll shows visitors at a Shinto shrine.

At larger shrines, a sacred white horse (or a statue of one) is offered as a gift to the *kami* each year.

A Japanese priest

WOW!

Zen is a special form of Buddhism practised in Japan. It involves a lot of meditation.

Mount Fuji's summit has a shrine to the Shinto goddess Sengen-Sama. The volcano itself was named after the Buddhist fire goddess, Fuchi.

MIX AND MATCH

When other belief systems, such as Buddhism and Christianity, were brought to Japan, people adopted those ideas too – but they also carried on following Shinto traditions. The different religions could exist side by side.

Revolutions

Until 1945, Japanese emperors were believed to be divine relatives of Amaterasu. No wonder their subjects obeyed them! Religion even influenced Japanese gardens. They mimic wild nature to bring people closer to kami.

ALL-POWERFUL GODS

The two most widely practised religions are Christianity and Islam. Both involve the worship of one god, not many. The prophet Abraham plays an important part in the main three monotheistic (single-God) religions - Judaism, Christianity and Islam. Sikhism, Zoroastrianism and the Baha'i Faith are monotheistic, too.

ONE VERSUS MANY

In a polytheistic society, there are so many gods and festivals that no one can worship or observe them all. As a result, people are often doing different things at the same time. A society with only one God is different. The rules are much clearer. Everyone in society does the same thing at the same time.

Jews refer to a book called a haggadah to make sure they celebrate the festival of Passover correctly, including its ritual meal, the Seder.

Guru Nanak founded Sikhism in what is now Pakistan in the 15th century CE. Sikhs believe in one God who made everything. They learn God's will from the ten gurus and from the Sikh holy book, the *Guru Granth Sahib*.

THE JEWISH FAITH

Judaism is one of the most ancient monotheistic faiths. Its followers, the Jews, trace their origins back to Abraham, whose name means 'a father of many nations'. Abraham was the first of the three Jewish patriarchs, or fathers. The other two are his son, Isaac, and Isaac's son, Jacob.

God tested Abraham by asking him to sacrifice his son, Isaac.

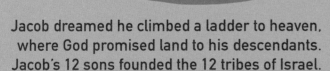

Jacob dreamed he climbed a ladder to heaven, where God promised land to his descendants. Jacob's 12 sons founded the 12 tribes of Israel.

NEED TO KNOW

VIP

David came from Bethlehem and was from the Tribe of Judah.

Saul was the first king to rule over the 12 Jewish tribes. He reigned during the 11th century BCE.

David was Israel's second king. He defeated the massive Philistine warrior, Goliath. He also made Jerusalem the Jewish capital.

David's son was Solomon. He was very wise, and he built the first Temple of Jerusalem.

The story of Judaism and its early leaders is told in the Hebrew Bible, or Torah (the Christian Old Testament). Muslims recognise many of the prophets, too.

King Solomon reading the Torah in a 13th-century Hebrew manuscript

The Torah begins with the Book of Genesis. This is the decorated first word in a Torah from around 1400.

WOW!

The Jewish language, Hebrew, is written from right to left.

Rabbi

PLACE OF WORSHIP

Jews go to the temple or synagogue to pray and to study the Torah. Spiritual teachers called rabbis guide them. Rabbis lead the worship at the synagogue and help people to interpret God's word.

Men and women sit in different places in the synagogue. This 15th-century Jewish prayer book shows men worshipping on Shabbat, the Jewish day of rest.

This 14th-century manuscript shows worshippers in a synagogue.

REVOLUTIONS

Strong faith and traditions helped the Jews to hold on to their identity even after they left their promised land and spread out across the world. This diaspora happened after their land became part of the Roman empire.

THE PROMISED LAND

One of the most powerful stories in Judaism tells how Moses led the Jews from Egypt to Canaan, the promised land. According to the story, the Jews were being kept as slaves in Egypt. During their time crossing the wilderness with Moses, they made an agreement, or covenant, with God.

God gave the Ten Commandments to Moses on the top of Mount Sinai in the Egyptian desert.

Moses and the Jews crossing the Red Sea, at the beginning of their journey from Egypt

Moses learned he was chosen to lead God's people when he saw a burning bush in the desert.

VIP

NEED TO KNOW

The pharaoh's daughter found Moses as a baby down by the Nile. His mother had hidden him there, because the pharaoh was killing all Jewish boys.

The adult Moses asked the pharaoh to free the Jews, but he refused. God sent ten terrible plagues on Egypt as punishment.

Egyptian soldiers pursued Moses and the Jews as they escaped from Egypt. But at the Red Sea God parted the waves so that only the Jews could cross.

Moses wrote down the Ten Commandments on two stone tablets.

THE TEN COMMANDMENTS

God gave Moses Ten Commandments – important, basic rules that all Jews must follow. In return, he promised they would reach Canaan.

WOW!

Moses never made it to the promised land. He died on the journey and Joshua took over as leader.

THE TABERNACLE

God told Moses to make a portable shrine, called the Tabernacle. It housed the Ark of the Covenant (the chest containing the commandments), an altar for incense, a table for offering bread to God and a lampstand called a menorah.

The menorah was a golden stand that held seven oil lamps. God gave Moses instructions how to make it.

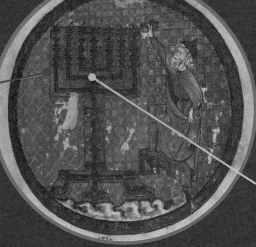

The middle branch represents God's light; the other six branches represent human wisdom.

When the Temple in Jerusalem was built, centuries later, the Tabernacle was put inside.

REVOLUTIONS

The Jewish promised land became a reality after World War II when the state of Israel was founded. However, just like long ago, other people lay claim to the same territory. There are clashes in the region.

▷▷▷▷▷▷▷▷▷▷▷▷▷▷▷▷

THE BIRTH OF CHRISTIANITY

Christians believe that Jesus Christ was not only a Jewish man, but also the Son of God. They believe he was sent to forgive people's sins, restore them to God and establish God's kingdom on Earth. They also believe Jesus was brought back to life after his death on the cross.

Christ was crucified (put to death by being nailed to a cross). Christians believe he died for people's sins.

This 16th-century image of Christ on the cross was painted by the Croatian artist Giulio Clovio.

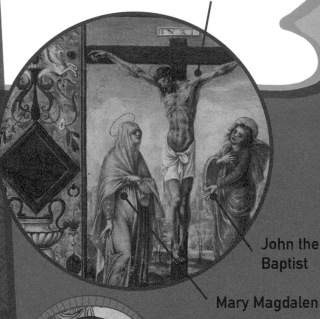

John the Baptist

Mary Magdalen

VIP

Matthew wrote the first gospel of the New Testament. The others were written by Mark, Luke and John.

NEED TO KNOW

The Torah, which Christians call the Old Testament, promises a Messiah — a king sent by God who will establish God's kingdom on Earth.

The New Testament contains gospels — accounts of Christ's life — written by four of his disciples (followers). They helped to spread Christ's teachings.

Christ is thought to have lived from around **4** BCE to **30** or **33** CE. At that time, the Jewish territories of Galilee and Judea were part of the Roman empire.

BABY JESUS

Incarnation means 'in the flesh'. The gospels explain that Christ was made flesh by being born to a young woman called Mary. The disciples' accounts show how his birth mattered to all layers of society – from lowly shepherds to important kings from the East. Matthew tells how Herod, the king of Judea, tried to have the infant Jesus killed.

WOW!

Herod was a true historical figure and so was Pontius Pilate, the Roman governor of Judea who sentenced Jesus to death.

BEYOND THE RESURRECTION

According to the New Testament, Jesus came back to life and left his tomb three days after his death on the cross. Forty days after that, his body went back up to heaven to be with God. The last book of the New Testament says the world will end in an apocalypse. Evil will be destroyed and Jesus will appear on a cloud in all his glory.

A monk in a Spanish monastery painted this vision of Christ after the apocalypse more than 900 years ago.

REVOLUTIONS

Without Christ and his teachings, there would be no Christianity. The Romans eventually converted to Christianity and their capital, Rome, became the centre of the Christian world.

XXXXXXXXXXXXXXXXXX

CHRISTIAN LIFE

For Christians, Jesus Christ is part of a Holy Trinity. The three parts – God the Father, God the Son and God the Holy Spirit – make up God as a whole. Most Christians follow their religion by worshipping in church and praying at home. Some decide to live religious lives as monks or nuns.

God the Son (Jesus)

God the Father

God the Holy Spirit (a dove)

Dominican nuns (followers of St Dominic)

A representation of the Trinity in a 15th-century *Book of Hours*

 VIP

St Benedict lived in Italy from around 480 CE to 547 CE.

NEED TO KNOW

Benedictine monks live in monasteries and spend time praying, studying and doing physical work. They follow the Rule of St Benedict, written around **540** CE.

By the time of St Francis of Assisi (c. **1181** to **1226**), many monasteries were very rich. Francis believed monks and nuns should live in poverty and preach.

Spanish priest St Dominic was another who thought monks should not stay shut up in monasteries but go out into the world. He founded the Dominicans in **1216**.

KEY MOMENTS

Christians mark important moments in their lives with rituals and church ceremonies that bring them closer to God. Priests lead these events.

Christian babies are baptised – splashed with water to symbolise being born again before God.

During a marriage service, the priest joins the bride and groom together before God.

WOW!

Christianity is the biggest organised religion, with more than 2.1 billion followers worldwide.

BREAD AND WINE

Holy communion is a ritual that happens during some church services. It helps Christians to remember the night before the crucifixion. At his Last Supper, Jesus asked the disciples to eat bread to remember his body and drink wine to remember his blood.

Monks ask God to bless bread and wine before holy communion (c. 1500).

REVOLUTIONS

Benedictine monks are responsible for some of our finest medieval books. Writing them out and hand-decorating them gave the monks a purpose. Christianity still gives many people structure and purpose.

THE BIRTH OF ISLAM

In 570 CE, the prophet Muhammad was born in in Mecca (now in Saudi Arabia). At the centre of the city was the Ka'aba, the black 'house' that Ibrahim and his son Ishmael had built for God. By Muhammad's time, it was full of pagan idols. God's messenger Jibrayil told Muhammad that there was only one God, Allah.

The Ka'aba

The Ka'aba in Mecca is the focus of Muslim worship. Muhammad cleansed it in 630 CE so it could be a shrine just for Allah.

Medina, where Muhammad died and spent most of the last ten years of his life

Mecca, where Muhammad was born and received his revelations from Allah

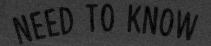

NEED TO KNOW

VIP Jibrayil (the Angel Gabriel in Judaism and Christianity) revealed God's word to Muhammad.

Muhammad came into conflict with the people of Mecca because he taught that there was only one God. In **622** CE, he and his followers had to move to Medina.

Between **622** and **630** CE, there were battles between the Meccans and Muslims. In **630** CE, Muhammad and his followers took control of Mecca.

Muhammad left a governor in charge of Mecca. By the time he died in Medina in **632** CE, the whole of the Arabian peninsula was Muslim.

HOLY BOOK

Allah's revelations to Muhammad were written down in the Qur'an. The holy book's central teaching is that there is only one God, Allah. It also gives instructions for every aspect of life and society.

A 16th-century Qur'an from Morocco

A 14th-century Qur'an from Mosul (now in Iraq)

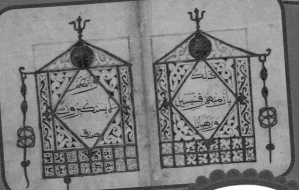

A 17th-century Qur'an from China

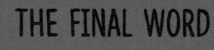

WOW!

Today, Islam is the second-largest religion, with around 1.5 billion followers worldwide.

THE FINAL WORD

According to the Qur'an, Muhammad is the last of a line of prophets who received messages from the one God. Earlier ones included Adam, Noah, Abraham, Moses and Jesus from the Jewish and Christian traditions.

Ibrahim (Abraham) is about to obey God's command and sacrifice Ismail (Isaac).

REVOLUTIONS

Muhammad's revelations formed the basis of the new religion of Islam. It rejected worshipping many gods and idols. Out of respect, Muslim artists did not directly show Allah or Muhammad. They glorified them with beautiful patterns and script instead.

MUSLIM LIFE

The Qur'an set out five duties that every Muslim must do. The first is to state that Allah is the only God. The others are worshipping daily, giving to charity, fasting and going on a pilgrimage at least once. These are the Five Pillars of Islam.

Muslims kneel on a prayer rug when they pray, either in the mosque or simply where they are when the call to prayer rings out.

Minaret (tower) points towards heaven

Muslims pray five times a day. The call to prayer comes from the top of the mosque's minaret.

 VIP Whirling dervishes are Sufis who perform trance-like dances.

NEED TO KNOW

The Qur'an is the central source of instruction for Muslims. They also refer to the Sunna (a description of Muhammad's life) and Hadith (a collection of his sayings).

Within **50** years of Muhammad's death, Muslims had split. Sunnis believed that the community should choose its leader. Shi'as thought Muslim leaders should be descendants of Muhammad.

Sufis live in poverty like some monks. They can be Sunni or Shi'a. They worship Allah through dance, song and drumming.

JOURNEY TO MECCA

Going on a hajj (pilgrimage to Mecca) is the fifth of the Pillars of Islam. Healthy Muslim men and women are expected to make the hajj at least once.

A caravan of pilgrims on the road to Mecca

WOW!

About two million Muslims make the pilgrimage to Mecca each year.

This beautiful document was given to a 15th-century pilgrim at Mecca as proof of her hajj.

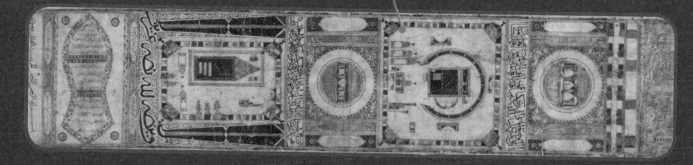

A procession to celebrate Eid-ul-Fitr in Delhi in the early 19th century

FASTS AND FEASTS

During the holy month of Ramadan, Muslims must go without food and drink during daylight hours. They end this fast with a celebration called Eid-ul-Fitr. It is the biggest festival of the Muslim year.

REVOLUTIONS

All Muslims believe that the Qur'an is the final word of God. In Islamic countries, scholars interpret the Qur'an to work out what the law should be. Islamic law is called Shari'a.

PHILOSOPHY AND IDEAS

Believing in a God or gods requires a leap of faith. Ideas based in science don't - they can be proved with evidence. Other kinds of thinking have changed human history, too, such as ideas about equality for everyone or what it means to be human.

POLITICAL CHANGE

Change can mean new ways of running society. There have been many different political systems over the years, each with its own values and methods for getting things done. Some are more successful than others. There is also the question of how to bring about change. Some activists believe that a peaceful, reasonable approach is the only option. Others use shock tactics or even acts of terrorism to achieve their aims.

Some campaigners for women's suffrage used extreme techniques. This British poster represents the suffragists, who always used peaceful and lawful means.

Mahatma Gandhi used peaceful protest to win Indian independence from Britain.

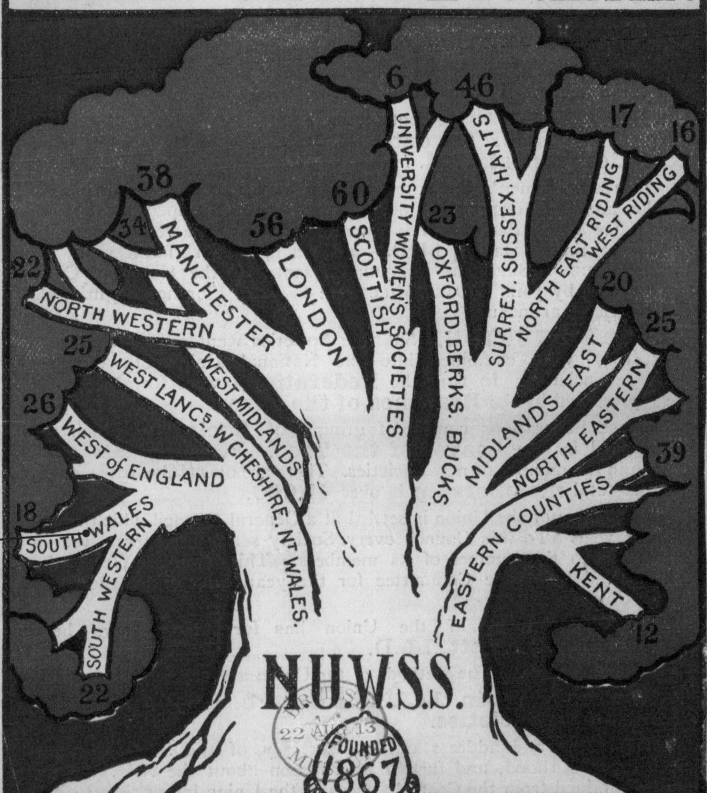

NATIONAL UNION
OF
WOMENS SUFFRAGE SOCIETIES.

N.U.W.S.S.

FOUNDED 1867

THE MEANING OF LIFE

The earliest Western philosophers were ancient Greeks, such as Socrates, Plato and Aristotle. As well as studying knowledge itself, they examined what it meant to exist and looked at the difference between the mind and the body. They explored tricky ideas such as beauty, truth, and right or wrong.

This Roman mosaic from the 1st century BCE shows Plato teaching philosophy in Athens.

This 19th-century painting shows an after-dinner discussion about what love meant. Plato wrote about this in his book, the *Symposium*.

Plato's Symposium by Anselm Feuerbach (1869)

This might be the boy Plato

Socrates

NEED TO KNOW

VIP Socrates lived in Athens between around 470 BCE and 399 BCE.

Socrates is sometimes called the father of Western philosophy. He thought that the best way to get closer to truth and ideas was through careful questioning.

By comparing the answers to different questions, Socrates showed that you could prove or disprove certain statements.

This clever technique for pinning down the truth is called the Socratic method. Socrates used it with his student, Plato. Their question-and-answer sessions are called dialogues.

THE STORY OF THE CAVE

One of Plato's most powerful ideas came from a story about prisoners chained up in a cave. They can see shadows on the wall of the cave, cast by puppets. A freed prisoner who could go outside the cave and see the Sun would come to understand that the outside world (not the shadows) was 'real'.

The prisoners do not know that the puppets or the fire exist. For them, the shadows are reality.

WOW!

Aristotle thought that everything in the world was made up of the following four elements: earth, water, fire and air.

FAMOUS PHILOSOPHER

The greatest student at Plato's Academy in Athens was Aristotle (384 BCE to 322 BCE). Like his teacher, he used logic to rule out certain ways of seeing the world and to form a truer picture. Aristotle also thought it was important to understand why things were the way they were

This 17th-century etching shows Aristotle receiving the key to knowledge – being able to reason.

The figure of the woman represents Wisdom.

REVOLUTIONS

The Western way of thinking owes everything to these early Greeks. They came up with a 'scientific' method for understanding the world

REVOLUTIONARY IDEAS

The Frenchman René Descartes is sometimes called the father of modern philosophy in the West. His most famous saying is *cogito ergo sum* ("I think, therefore I am"). For Descartes, the very act of thinking was proof of his own existence. His writings mark the start of a time called the Age of Reason.

Descartes' use of Reason was influenced by the scientific revolution – leaps forward in scientific understanding that had taken place in the 16th and 17th centuries.

Newton's diagram explaining gravity

In 1687, Isaac Newton put forward new ideas about the forces at work in the Universe.

VIP In the time of Isaac Newton (1643—1727), science was called natural philosophy.

NEED TO KNOW

Scientists such as Isaac Newton always searched for evidence to support their discoveries. Nothing could be guesswork any more.

Descartes' work marks the start of the Age of Reason or the Enlightenment — a time in Europe when thinkers questioned religion and championed science.

Enlightenment ideas led people to question old ideas of power and order. In France and North America, there were revolutions.

REASON AND THE MIND

Enlightenment thinkers believed that humans had certain natural rights. Aristotle had said something similar, so this was not a new idea. But in the 18th century it led people to question the control of kings and emperors.

The French Revolution took place between 1789 and 1799.

WOW!

The founding ideals of the French republic were liberty, equality and brotherhood.

THE ROMANTICS

Later in the 18th century some artists and thinkers began to rebel against being sensible and rational. The Romantics believed that scientific explanations missed out an important part of being human – feeling strong emotions.

Romantic composers such as the German Richard Wagner (1813–1883) made music that was full of feeling.

English painter and poet William Blake (1757–1827) was one of the early Romantic poets.

REVOLUTIONS

While thinking about what it meant to be human, Enlightenment philosophers defined certain human rights. Many of these are part of today's Charter of Human Rights.

VOTES (AND MORE) FOR WOMEN

The Parisian playwright Olympe de Gouges believed in equality. In 1789, she joined the French Revolution to topple Louis XVI ... but then she read her fellow-revolutionaries' *Declaration of the Rights of Man*. It called only for men's rights, not women's.

Marriage was just one of many areas of 18th-century life where men had more rights than women. De Gouges argued against marriage in her *Rights of Woman* in 1791.

De Gouges's ideas were threatening to many men. She was executed by guillotine in 1793.

NEED TO KNOW

Mary Wollstonecraft's *Rights of Women* was published in 1792.

Few girls had proper schooling in the **18**th century. British thinker Mary Wollstonecraft believed the best path to equality was for girls to be educated.

A wife's property automatically belonged to her husband when they married. In the **19**th century, countries such as the UK and USA passed laws to alter this.

In **1867**, English philosopher John Stuart Mill tried to change the law so that women could vote in elections. His suggestion was laughed out of parliament.

PIONEERS

By the early 20th century, many brave men and women were campaigning for women's suffrage (being able to vote). Some worked peacefully. Others drew attention to the cause with shocking acts such as hunger strikes, arson and stone throwing.

Suffragette brooch

Green for hope

Purple for dignity

White for purity

Suffragettes wear placards to advertise a public meeting.

WOW!

Suffragette Emily Davison died after throwing herself in front of the king's horse in June 1913.

Will you help the Women of France?

SAVE WHEAT

CHANGING TIMES

The outbreak of World War I helped to bring change more quickly. With so many men away fighting, women had to do men's jobs. They were proving their equality every day.

A poster encouraging women to be thrifty with food because it took so much work to farm it

From 1917, women worked for Britain's air force, the Royal Flying Corps.

REVOLUTIONS

New Zealand was the first country to give women the vote, in 1893. American women won the vote in 1920 and all British women by 1928. During the 20th century women took on more traditionally male jobs. However, even into the 21st century they were often still paid less than men.

CIVIL RIGHTS

Slavery was abolished in the United States in 1865, but nearly a century later African-Americans were still not receiving equal treatment. In some states there was segregation (separate areas for blacks and whites) in many public spaces, from buses and schools to parks, restaurants and hotels.

In August 1963, more than 250,000 civil rights activists marched on Washington.

There were separate water fountains for white and black people.

VIP

Martin Luther King Jr headed the struggle for civil rights from 1957 until his assassination in 1968.

NEED TO KNOW

In **1954**, Reverend Oliver Brown of Springfield, Missouri, won the right to send his daughter to a white school. In **1957**, nine black students attending a school in Little Rock, Arkansas, needed army protection.

Martin Luther King Jr gave his "I have a dream..." speech at the Washington March in **1963**. It spelled out his hopes for equality in the future.

In **1964**, the US government outlawed segregation. In **1965**, all African-Americans were given the vote.

THE MONTGOMERY BUS BOYCOTT

In 1955, Rosa Parks was arrested in Montgomery, Alabama, for refusing to give up her bus seat to a white man. The front seats were reserved for white people. In response, fellow African-Americans refused to use any of Montgomery's buses until segregation ended a year later.

Rosa Parks

Barack Obama

Barack Obama was the USA's first African-American president. He served from 2009 to 2017.

SOUTH AFRICA'S STORY

In South Africa, segregation was the law from 1948 to 1994. It was called apartheid (meaning 'separateness'). Black people were not allowed to vote and mixed marriages between whites and blacks were banned. Protestors were imprisoned.

CONDEMN THE SOUTH AFRICAN APARTHEID REGIME AND SUPPORT THE INTERNATIONAL BOYCOTT

Boycotts put pressure on South Africa to end apartheid.

Nelson Mandela was jailed for 27 years for his activism in the 1960s. In 1994, he became South Africa's first black president.

A cell in the prison on Robben Island where many anti-apartheid protestors were imprisoned, including Mandela.

REVOLUTIONS

It is only just over 50 years since segregation ended in the USA and 20 years since the end of apartheid in South Africa. In many countries, people from ethnic minorities still suffer from discrimination, even where laws protect against racism.

THE PATH OF EVOLUTION

From 1831 to 1836, a young scientist called Charles Darwin travelled on HMS *Beagle*. The ship was surveying South America and Australia, and its captain had employed Darwin to help collect and document plant and animal specimens along the way.

This illustration of the 62-year-old Darwin appeared in *Vanity Fair* magazine.

HMS *Beagle* off the coast of Chile

Darwin discovered bones of an extinct giant ground sloth, *Mylodon darwinii*, in Argentina.

Mount Sarmiento, which Darwin described as a 'sublime spectacle'

VIP English scientist Alfred Russel Wallace came up with his theory of natural selection at the same time as Darwin.

NEED TO KNOW

French scientist Georges Cuvier was one of the first to explain fossils of extinct animals in **1813**. He believed that every so often huge floods wiped out all the existing species.

On the *Beagle* in the **1830s**, Darwin encountered different but similar species. They convinced him that natural selection makes species change, or evolve, over time.

Darwin published his theory of evolution in his great work, *On the Origin of Species*, in **1859**.

SCIENCE SPLIT

Darwin's ideas caused an outcry. People worried that his theory went against the story of creation in the Bible. However, a few scientists supported Darwin's ideas. By the 1870s, they were accepted as fact by most people.

This drawing appeared in a book by Thomas Huxley in 1863. It showed similarities between ape and human skeletons.

Thomas Huxley was one of the scientists who supported Darwin's ideas.

WOW!

More than 250 species are named after Charles Darwin.

AGE OF THE DINOSAURS

At the same time as Darwin was writing, huge discoveries were being made about dinosaurs. New fossils were being found, and new explanations for how dinosaurs had lived and why they had died.

Iguanodon

Megalosaurus, the first dinosaur to be named

This illustration was published in 1865.

Richard Owen coined the name dinosaur, meaning 'terrible lizard', in 1842.

REVOLUTIONS

Darwin is one of the most influential people in history. His ideas revolutionised the fields of biology, zoology and botany. They changed how people thought about God and where we come from.

THE BIGGER PICTURE

For most of our human history, myths and religious stories have explained our place in the Universe. In modern times, science has offered explanations. Is science the only reality or is it further proof of the greatness of godly powers?

People used to believe that Earth was at the centre of the Universe. This is called the Ptolemaic system, after Greek-Egyptian astronomer Ptolemy, who lived in the 2nd century CE.

Christianity and other religions offered a divine explanation for the movement of the stars and planets.

NEED TO KNOW

VIP

Italian astronomer Galileo Galilei was the first to view space through a telescope in 1610.

Polish astronomer Nicolaus Copernicus rejected the Ptolemaic system in **1543**. He put forward a system with the Sun at the centre instead.

The invention of the telescope in **1608** meant that astronomers could see farther into space than ever before.

The first space telescopes were launched in the **1970s**. They have given us excellent views of space beyond our solar system.

LIFE AND TIMES

From the 19th century, writers began to explore ideas such as time travel and the possibility of life on other worlds. Science fiction was born. During the 20th century, some of these concepts became science fact.

The War of the Worlds, published in 1898, described an invasion by hostile Martians. This illustration is from a 1906 edition of the book.

WOW!

A 1938 radio broadcast of the War of the Worlds caused panic. It was in the style of a news story — and listeners thought it was true!

In his theories of relativity, Albert Einstein showed that time is not fixed. It can slow down.

In the 1960s, scientists saw the first microwave images of cosmic background radiation. These show energy rippling out after the Big Bang.

BIG BANG

During the 1920s, physicists began to suggest the idea of an expanding Universe. It seemed likely that all the matter and energy in the Universe was created in a huge explosion. Today we call that event the Big Bang and have evidence that it happened 13.7 billion years ago.

REVOLUTIONS

The Universe is expanding, and so is our concept of it. The scientific story holds together, but there are unexplained gaps ... scientists talk about concepts such as 'dark matter' to make the data fit. Perhaps they will identify what this is, or perhaps there is a whole new reality out there to be explained.

GLOSSARY

afterlife
Life after death, often in another world, such as heaven or the underworld.

astronomy
The study of the stars and planets and their movements.

avatar
A god in bodily form.

caste system
A way of grouping Indian society according to class and skin colour.

civil rights
Rights such as the freedom to vote that have to be enforced by law.

civilisation
A settled society that has developed a form of government, writing, organised religion, trade and great buildings.

Communist
A believer in Communism, a way of organising society so that there is no private property.

covenant
An agreement or contract between God and his people.

cremate
To burn a dead person's body.

demigod
Half-god and half-mortal.

demon
An evil spirit or devil.

diaspora
The spreading out of a people away from their homeland, especially of the Jews away from Israel.

divine
Relating or referring to God or gods.

embalm
To preserve a dead body with salts to prevent it from decaying.

empire
A group of lands or peoples brought under the rule of one person (emperor) or government.

enlightenment
A state of being aware of the true nature of human existence and how to end suffering.

evolve
To change slowly over time.

immortal
Describes someone who will live forever.

mantra
A sound or word that is repeated to aid meditation.

meditation
The act of sitting and thinking about something deeply.

monotheism
Belief in one God.

natural selection
The process that drives evolution by favouring organisms that are best suited to their surroundings and therefore making them more likely to survive and pass on their genes.

nirvana
A state of peace and enlightenment, achieved by escaping the desires of the world.

Norse
A Scandinavian person in medieval times, such as a Viking.

oracle bones
Bones used in ancient China to seek knowledge of the future.

Philistines
An ancient people who settled what is now the Middle East around the 12th century BCE.

philosophy
The study of existence and the meaning of life.

pilgrimage
A journey to a holy place by a religious follower.

polytheism
Belief in many gods.

prophet
Someone through whom God speaks.

republic
A country without a king or queen.

ritual
A ceremony in which the order of events and the words used rarely change over the years.

segregation
The separation of different races.

shaman
A person who can communicate with the spirit world.

shrine
A sacred building or place, often housing a holy object.

slave
A person who is held as the property of another.

spirit
A person or being without a body.

stupa
A dome-shaped building that is a Buddhist shrine.

suffragette
A woman seeking the right to vote.

tribe
A group of people who are often related and share the same language and culture.

trickster
A character who cheats or deceives others.

INDEX

CREDITS

a = above, **b** = below, **c** = centre, **l** = left, **r** = right
All images © The British Library Board except:
Back cover - Totem pole: Peter Graham, Stanley Park, Vancouver; Suffragettes, Martin Luther King: Library of Congress, Washington D.C.; Red Fuji: Private Collection.
Glenbow Museum, Alberta: 23a; Michael Fu: 57b; Alexey Gaponov: 23b; Glasgow Women's Library: 55al; Peter Graham, Stanley Park, Vancouver: 23r; National Maritime Museum, Greenwich: 60b; Staatliche Kunsthalle, Karlsruhe: 50l; Árne Magnússon Institute for Icelandic Studies: 12l; Markus Maurer: 51a; NASA: 61b; Marie-Lan Nguyen/Museo Nazionale Archeologico, Naples: 50a; Musée du Louvre, Paris: 53a; Private Collection: 13b, 16a, 33b, 54ar; Reggaeman: 32l; Teseum: 19b; Centraal Museum, Utrecht: 52a; National Library of Austria, Vienna: 61c; University of Virginia Library: 58ar; Library of Congress, Washington D.C.: 55a, 56, 57al, 57ar (Photo Pete Souza), 57cr (Photo Maureen Keating), 57cl (Rachel Romero); Wellcome Images: 31b, 51b, 59a; www.123rf: 9b, 46l.

Hand-drawn design elements: Shutterstock, with thanks to AuraLux, Bisams, eaxx, Franzi, Krolia and Skokan Olena.
Typeset in Agent 'C' by Carl Leisegang, Lazing on a Sunny Afternoon by Frédéric Rich, Petit Four by Hanoded, Gochi Hand by Huerta Tipográfica, La Belle Aurore by Kimberly Geswein and DIN Alternate.